# ABRAHAM & ISAAC

## THE CALL OF A CHOSEN MAN

### THOMAS ALLEN

portion of this book is strictly prohibited and may result in legal action. Any person found to be in violation of these terms may be subject to civil and/or criminal penalties, including fines and imprisonment.

If you are considering pirating or copying this book, know that you will be violating the law and that there will be

consequences. The author and publisher take intellectual property theft very seriously and will pursue all legal

remedies available to them. Don't risk your freedom and financial stability by engaging in illegal activity. Instead,

support the hard work and creativity of the author by purchasing a legitimate copy of this book.

## Governing Law:

This book is governed by the laws of the country in which it is purchased. Any legal disputes arising from the use

or distribution of this book shall be subject to the exclusive jurisdiction of the courts in that country.

## Disclaimer Notice:

Please note the information contained within this document is for educational and entertainment purposes only.

All effort has been executed to present accurate, up-to-date, reliable, and complete information. No warranties of

any kind are declared or implied. Readers acknowledge that the author is not engaged in the rendering of legal,

financial, medical, or professional advice. The content within this book has been derived from various sources.

Please consult a licensed professional before attempting any techniques outlined in this book. By reading this document, the reader agrees that under no circumstances is the author responsible for any losses,

direct or indirect, that are incurred as a result of the use of the information contained within this document, including, but not limited to, errors, omissions, or inaccuracies.

# Table of Contents

# Introduction

## A Covenant with God

### The Call of a Chosen Man

In a world of shifting sands and fleeting kingdoms, one man stood apart. Abraham, a man of humble beginnings, was called by God to leave behind everything he knew—his homeland, his family, and the life he had built. God's voice broke through the ordinary, offering an extraordinary promise:

**"Go to the land I will show you, and I will make you into a great nation. I will bless you and make your name great, and you will be a blessing."**

With nothing but faith in this divine command, Abraham set out into the unknown. His journey was not without trials—famine, conflict, and doubt shadowed his steps. Yet, with each altar he built and every prayer he offered, Abraham's trust in God deepened. His life became a testament to obedience and hope in promises not yet fulfilled.

### The Promise of a Son

Central to God's covenant was the promise of descendants as numerous as the stars. But for Abraham and his wife, Sarah, this seemed impossible. Their advanced age and years of barrenness made the prospect of a child almost laughable. Yet God's word remained steadfast:

**"Sarah, your wife, will bear you a son, and you will call him Isaac. Through him, my covenant will be established."**

Against all odds, Sarah conceived, and Isaac was born—a child of joy and laughter, the embodiment of God's faithfulness. Isaac's birth was not just a personal blessing but the fulfillment of a promise that stretched across generations.

### A Life Defined by Tests

Abraham's journey of faith was marked by trials, each one refining his trust in God. From leaving his homeland to navigating the tensions between his sons, Ishmael and Isaac, Abraham's life was one of surrender to divine will.

But no test would challenge him as deeply as the one to come. The God who had promised Abraham countless descendants would now ask for the unthinkable: the sacrifice of Isaac, the child of promise. It was a command that defied reason and pierced the very heart of Abraham's faith.

## The Weight of Obedience

When the command came, Abraham was silent. He did not question or argue, but the weight of God's request pressed heavily on his spirit. How could he reconcile the love he held for his son with the obedience he owed to his Creator? How could the fulfillment of God's covenant require such a loss?

The journey to Mount Moriah would test not only Abraham's faith but also his humanity. It would force him to confront the depths of his trust in God and the limits of his understanding.

## An Invitation to Reflect

The story of Abraham and Isaac is not just an ancient tale; it is a timeless exploration of faith, love, and sacrifice. It invites us to grapple with the complexities of trust in a higher purpose, even when it challenges our deepest desires and understanding.

As you journey through this retelling, step into the shoes of Abraham, a father torn between his love for his son and his unwavering faith in God. Walk alongside Isaac, a child whose trust in his father and his Creator is both innocent and profound. And consider the enduring themes of obedience, provision, and the unshakable power of God's promises.

This is the story of Abraham and Isaac—a story of faith tested, love surrendered, and a covenant that would shape the destiny of nations.

# Chapter One

## Abraham's Call

### The Voice in the Wilderness

It was an ordinary day in Haran, the sun casting its golden glow across the dry plains as Abraham tended to his herds. The steady rhythm of his life was interrupted by a voice, one that carried an authority beyond human comprehension.

**"Leave your country, your people, and your father's household, and go to the land I will show you. I will make you into a great nation, and I will bless you. I will make your name great, and you will be a blessing."**

Abraham froze, his heart pounding. This was the voice of the Creator, the One who had set the stars in place and breathed life into humanity. The words were clear, but their implications were vast. Leave everything he knew? Venture into the unknown? Yet, there was a promise—one that stirred something deep within him: the promise of blessing, legacy, and purpose.

### The Decision to Obey

The command demanded more than physical movement; it required surrender. Abraham would have to leave his comfort, his kin, and his plans for the future.

When he shared the call with his wife, Sarah, her brow furrowed in concern. **"Leave Haran? But where will we go?"**

**"I do not know,"** Abraham admitted. **"But the One who spoke to me will guide us. He has promised to make of us a great nation."**

Sarah's eyes softened. She knew Abraham's faith was unwavering, and despite her fears, she agreed to follow him. They gathered their belongings, their servants, and their livestock. Alongside his nephew, Lot, Abraham began his journey, leaving the familiarity of Haran behind.

### The Challenges of the Journey

The road ahead was difficult, marked by harsh terrain, unpredictable weather, and the uncertainties of the unknown. Days stretched into weeks as they traveled through barren landscapes and distant towns. Each step required trust, each mile a reminder of their dependence on God's guidance.

At times, doubt whispered in Abraham's mind. **"What if I've misunderstood? What if this journey leads nowhere?"** But each evening, as the stars filled the heavens, he was reminded of the promise: descendants as numerous as those lights in the sky.

Abraham built altars at each place they camped, offering sacrifices and prayers. These altars became markers of his journey, physical symbols of his faith in God's direction.

### The Land of Canaan

At last, they arrived in the land of Canaan, a place of rolling hills and fertile plains. The Creator spoke again, reaffirming the promise:

**"To your offspring, I will give this land."**

Abraham stood in awe, his heart swelling with gratitude and anticipation. He built another altar, dedicating the land and his journey to God. Though he did not yet see how the promise would be fulfilled, he trusted in the One who had called him.

### Trials and Tests

Life in Canaan was not without challenges. A severe famine forced Abraham to seek refuge in Egypt, where deception and fear tested his faith. Later, disputes arose between his herdsmen and Lot's, leading them to part ways. Abraham gave Lot the first choice of land, demonstrating his trust in God to provide.

Through every trial, Abraham's faith was refined. Each test reminded him that the promise was not dependent on his circumstances but on God's faithfulness.

### The Covenant Confirmed

One night, as Abraham looked up at the stars, the Creator spoke again:

**"Look up at the sky and count the stars—if indeed you can count them. So shall your offspring be."**

Abraham's heart swelled with belief, and the Creator sealed the covenant with him. Though he had no children yet, he trusted that God would fulfill His promise in His time.

### Closing the Chapter

Abraham's call marked the beginning of an extraordinary journey—one of faith, obedience, and trust in God's plan. Each step into the unknown brought him closer to understanding the depth of God's promises and the purpose for which he was chosen.

As the stars shone over Canaan, Abraham's resolve grew stronger. His faith was not without doubt or struggle, but it was unwavering in its foundation: a trust in the Creator who had called him to a purpose beyond his understanding.

# Chapter Two

## The Promise of Isaac

### Waiting for the Promise

Years passed in Canaan, and though the land was abundant and Abraham's flocks grew, the fulfillment of God's promise seemed distant. The absence of a child weighed heavily on Abraham and Sarah. Despite God's assurance, the years of barrenness had left them weary with waiting.

One evening, as Abraham sat by the fire, gazing at the stars, Sarah approached him. Her face was lined with concern. **"The Lord has kept me from bearing children,"** she said. **"Perhaps you should take Hagar, my servant. She can bear a child for us."**

Abraham hesitated, but Sarah's desperation persuaded him. Hagar, the Egyptian servant, became pregnant, and soon Ishmael was born. Yet what seemed like a solution only brought strife.

### The Complications of Ishmael

Hagar's pregnancy created tension in the household. Sarah, once willing to share her husband for the sake of the promise, now felt resentment toward Hagar. The joy of Ishmael's birth was overshadowed by jealousy and conflict.

**"This was not God's plan,"** Abraham realized, his heart heavy. Ishmael, though beloved, was not the child through whom God had promised to fulfill the covenant.

Even so, Abraham loved Ishmael and prayed for him. God reassured Abraham: **"As for Ishmael, I have heard you; I will bless him and make him into a great nation. But my covenant will be established with Isaac, whom Sarah will bear to you by this time next year."**

### God Reaffirms the Promise

When Abraham was ninety-nine years old, God appeared to him again, reaffirming the covenant and changing his name from Abram to Abraham, meaning "father of many nations." Sarah's name was also changed, a sign of her pivotal role in the fulfillment of the promise.

**"I will bless Sarah and give you a son by her. She will be the mother of nations; kings of peoples will come from her,"** God declared.

Abraham fell facedown and laughed. **"Will a child be born to a man a hundred years old? Will Sarah bear a child at the age of ninety?"** he asked in disbelief. But the Creator's words were unwavering: Isaac would be born, and through him, the covenant would endure.

### Sarah's Laughter

Not long after, three visitors arrived at Abraham's tent. He welcomed them with the hospitality for which he was known, offering food and rest. As they ate, one of the visitors declared, **"By this time next year, Sarah, your wife, will have a son."**

Listening from the entrance of the tent, Sarah laughed quietly to herself. **"After I am worn out and my lord is old, will I now have this pleasure?"** she thought.

The visitor, who was none other than the Lord, asked, **"Why did Sarah laugh? Is anything too hard for the Lord?"** Sarah, startled, denied laughing, but the Lord's question lingered in her heart.

### The Joy of Fulfillment

True to God's word, Sarah conceived, and Isaac was born within the year. The laughter that had once been tinged with doubt was now filled with joy. Sarah held her son close, marveling at the miracle of his birth.

**"God has brought me laughter,"** she said, **"and everyone who hears about this will laugh with me."**

Isaac, whose name means "he laughs," became the living embodiment of God's faithfulness. The long years of waiting and doubt had culminated in a promise fulfilled.

### A Household Divided

Though Isaac's birth brought joy, it also deepened the tension in Abraham's household. Ishmael, now a young boy, mocked Isaac, stirring Sarah's protective instincts.

"Get rid of that slave woman and her son," Sarah demanded. "For that woman's son will never share in the inheritance with my son Isaac."

Abraham was distressed, torn between his love for Ishmael and his duty to Isaac. But God reassured him: "Do not be distressed. Listen to whatever Sarah tells you, because it is through Isaac that your offspring will be reckoned. I will make Ishmael into a nation as well, because he is your offspring."

With a heavy heart, Abraham sent Hagar and Ishmael away, trusting in God's promise to care for them.


### Closing the Chapter

The birth of Isaac marked the fulfillment of God's covenant with Abraham, but it also brought new challenges. The joy of the promise fulfilled was tempered by the complexities of family, faith, and the future.

Through it all, Abraham's trust in God deepened. He had seen the impossible become reality and knew that the Creator's promises, though sometimes delayed, were always certain. As he held Isaac, he felt the weight of God's faithfulness—and the promise of generations to come.

# Chapter Three

## The Command

### A Startling Command

Abraham's days were filled with the simple joys of fatherhood. Isaac, the child of promise, brought laughter and light to his aging parents. The boy's curious questions and boundless energy reminded Abraham daily of God's faithfulness.

But one morning, as the first rays of sunlight broke over the hills, Abraham heard God's voice again. This time, the words were unlike anything he had heard before.

**"Take your son, your only son, Isaac, whom you love, and go to the region of Moriah. Sacrifice him there as a burnt offering on a mountain I will show you."**

The weight of the command struck Abraham like a blow. Isaac was not just his son; he was the fulfillment of God's promise. How could the same God who had given this child now demand his life?

### A Father's Struggle

Abraham's heart was torn. The love he held for Isaac was immeasurable, but so too was his trust in God. The night after receiving the command, Abraham sat by the fire, staring into the flickering flames.

**"Why, Lord?"** he whispered into the silence. **"Why would You ask this of me?"**

There was no answer, but Abraham resolved to obey. He had seen God's faithfulness time and time again. Though he did not understand the command, he trusted that God's purpose was greater than his own understanding.

### The Journey to Moriah

Early the next morning, Abraham rose and saddled his donkey. He took Isaac and two servants with him, along with the wood for the burnt offering. As they set out, Abraham's steps were heavy, his heart burdened by the knowledge of what lay ahead.

For three days, they traveled in silence. Each mile felt like an eternity, the weight of the command pressing on Abraham's shoulders. Isaac, unaware of the true purpose of their journey, occasionally asked questions about the destination.

**"Father, where are we going?"** he asked, his voice filled with curiosity.

**"To worship,"** Abraham replied, his voice steady despite the turmoil in his heart.

### Isaac's Question

On the third day, Abraham looked up and saw the mountain in the distance. He stopped the servants and said, **"Stay here with the donkey while I and the boy go over there. We will worship, and then we will come back to you."**

Placing the wood for the burnt offering on Isaac's shoulders, Abraham carried the fire and the knife. As they climbed the mountain, Isaac spoke again.

**"Father?"**

**"Yes, my son?"**

**"The fire and wood are here,"** Isaac said, **"but where is the lamb for the burnt offering?"**

Abraham's throat tightened, but he forced himself to speak. **"God Himself will provide the lamb for the burnt offering, my son."**

Isaac nodded, satisfied with the answer, and they continued in silence.

### Building the Altar

When they reached the place God had shown him, Abraham built an altar and arranged the wood on it. Each stone he placed felt heavier than the last, each movement deliberate and reverent.

Finally, he turned to Isaac. **"My son,"** he said, his voice trembling. **"Come here."**

Isaac's eyes widened as realization dawned, but he did not resist. The trust between father and son, forged over years of love and guidance, held firm. With tears in his eyes, Abraham bound Isaac and placed him on the altar.

### The Ultimate Test

Abraham reached for the knife, his hand shaking as he raised it above his son. The moment seemed to stretch into eternity, the silence broken only by the sound of his labored breathing.

Just as he prepared to strike, a voice called out from heaven. **"Abraham! Abraham!"**

He froze, the knife poised in the air. **"Here I am,"** he replied, his voice a mixture of relief and desperation.

**"Do not lay a hand on the boy,"** the voice said. **"Do not do anything to him. Now I know that you fear God, because you have not withheld from Me your son, your only son."**

### God's Provision

Abraham lowered the knife, his entire body trembling with emotion. He untied Isaac, who clung to his father, his trust unshaken despite the ordeal.

Looking up, Abraham saw a ram caught in a thicket by its horns. With a heart full of gratitude, he took the ram and sacrificed it as a burnt offering instead of his son.

Abraham named the place **"The Lord Will Provide,"** saying, **"On the mountain of the Lord, it will be provided."**

### The Covenant Reaffirmed

As the smoke of the offering rose into the sky, the angel of the Lord called to Abraham again.

**"I swear by Myself, declares the Lord, that because you have done this and have not withheld your son, your only son, I will surely bless you and make your descendants as numerous as the stars in the sky and as the sand on the seashore. Through your offspring, all nations on earth will be blessed, because you have obeyed Me."**

Abraham's heart swelled with relief and gratitude. The test, though incomprehensible, had deepened his faith and reaffirmed God's promise.

### Closing the Chapter

Abraham and Isaac descended the mountain together, the bond between them stronger than ever. The journey had been one of unimaginable pain, but it had also revealed the depth of Abraham's faith and the certainty of God's provision.

# Chapter Four

## The Aftermath

### Returning Home

The journey back from Mount Moriah was quiet. Abraham and Isaac walked side by side, their steps steady but their hearts heavy with reflection. For Abraham, the experience had solidified his trust in God, but it had also left an indelible mark on his soul. Isaac, though young, carried the weight of the event in silence, his trust in his father and in God unshaken but deeply shaped by what had transpired.

When they reached the camp, Sarah greeted them with relief, though a shadow of concern crossed her face as she noticed their solemn expressions. Abraham embraced her, the weight of the journey's events too profound to put into words. For now, the details would remain between him, Isaac, and God.

### Isaac's Quiet Transformation

Isaac's demeanor changed in the days that followed. The childlike exuberance he once carried was tempered by a new depth of understanding. He often sat quietly, staring at the horizon, as if contemplating the events on Mount Moriah.

One evening, as they watched the stars, Isaac turned to Abraham. **"Father, do you think God will ask me to make such a sacrifice someday?"**

Abraham's heart ached at the question. **"I do not know, my son. But I do know this: God is faithful. He will never ask more of us than He provides for. You were never alone on that mountain, Isaac. The Lord was with us."**

Isaac nodded, the answer enough for now. The bond between father and son grew deeper, forged in the fire of faith and trust.

### The Community's Reaction

As the story of what happened on Mount Moriah spread, it stirred mixed reactions among Abraham's household and the surrounding community. Some marveled at Abraham's faith, seeing him as a man completely devoted to God's will. Others whispered doubts, questioning how a father could be willing to sacrifice his son.

Abraham's response was simple. **"The Lord provides,"** he said to those who asked. **"His ways are higher than ours. I trusted Him, and He proved faithful."**

### God's Reaffirmed Blessing

The events on Mount Moriah marked a turning point in Abraham's journey with God. The covenant was no longer just a promise—it was a reality lived and tested. God's words on the mountain echoed in Abraham's heart:

**"Through your offspring, all nations on earth will be blessed."**

Abraham began to see the covenant not just as a promise to his family, but as a mission for all of humanity. The generations to come would carry the legacy of faith, trust, and obedience.

### The Legacy of the Altar

The altar on Mount Moriah became a symbol of God's provision and faithfulness. Though Abraham and Isaac never returned to the site, its memory remained vivid in their minds. Isaac, in particular, often spoke of the altar as a place where he learned the true meaning of trust.

As Isaac grew, he carried the lessons of Mount Moriah into his own life. The God who provided the ram would become the foundation of his own faith, shaping the choices he would make and the family he would lead.

### Sarah's Reflection

For Sarah, the story of Mount Moriah was both unsettling and affirming. She struggled to reconcile the idea of a God who would ask such a sacrifice with the One who had fulfilled His promise by giving her Isaac. But as she watched Isaac thrive and Abraham's faith deepen, she came to understand the lesson of the altar.

**"God's ways are not ours,"** she told herself. **"But His faithfulness is sure."**

### A Lesson for Generations

The story of Abraham and Isaac became more than a family memory—it was a narrative passed down through the generations. Each retelling emphasized the themes of obedience, trust, and God's provision. It was a story not of despair, but of hope, reminding future generations of the covenant that bound them to God.

The phrase **"The Lord Will Provide"** became a cornerstone of their faith, a reminder that even in the darkest moments, God's provision would shine through.

### Closing the Chapter

The aftermath of Mount Moriah was not just the conclusion of a test—it was the beginning of a legacy. Abraham's unwavering faith and Isaac's quiet trust would echo through history, shaping the story of a people chosen to carry God's promise.

# Chapter Five

## The Continuation of the Promise

### Life After the Test

Life in Abraham's camp settled into a rhythm after the events on Mount Moriah. The memory of the test lingered, shaping Abraham's interactions with his family and strengthening his faith. His relationship with Isaac deepened, their bond forged in trust and love. For Abraham, each day was a testament to God's mercy and the certainty of His promises.

Sarah, too, found peace in the years that followed. The joy of watching Isaac grow into a young man softened the weight of her earlier doubts. She often marveled at the laughter and life her son brought to the camp, a constant reminder of God's faithfulness.

### Isaac's Role in the Covenant

As Isaac matured, Abraham began to teach him the full scope of the covenant. Sitting under the stars, they spoke of God's promises—the countless descendants, the land of Canaan, and the mission to bless all nations.

**"Isaac,"** Abraham said one night, **"you are not just my son. You are the child of the covenant. Through you, God's promise will be fulfilled. It is a heavy responsibility, but you do not carry it alone. The Lord will guide you."**

Isaac listened intently, the weight of his father's words settling in his heart. Though young, he understood that his life was part of something far greater than himself.

### The Passing of Sarah

The joy of their growing family was tempered by loss when Sarah passed away at the age of 127. Her death marked the end of an era for Abraham, who mourned deeply for his wife. She had been his companion through every trial, from leaving their homeland to the birth of Isaac.

Abraham purchased the cave of Machpelah as a burial site, ensuring Sarah had a resting place in the land God had promised. This act not only honored Sarah's memory but also reaffirmed Abraham's trust in the covenant. The land was more than soil—it was part of the divine promise to his descendants.

### A Bride for Isaac

As Isaac grew older, Abraham turned his thoughts to securing a future for his son. Knowing the covenant would pass through Isaac, he resolved to find a wife for him—not from the Canaanites, but from among his own people.

Abraham called for his most trusted servant and said, **"Go to my homeland and find a wife for my son Isaac. The Lord will send His angel before you to guide your way."**

The servant traveled to Mesopotamia and prayed for guidance at a well. There, he met Rebekah, a woman of kindness and faith, who offered water not only to him but also to his camels. Convinced that God had led him to her, the servant brought Rebekah back to Canaan.

### The Marriage of Isaac and Rebekah

When Isaac saw Rebekah for the first time, his heart was moved. The marriage was one of love and purpose, uniting them in the mission of the covenant. Rebekah, like Sarah before her, became a vital part of God's plan, her faith complementing Isaac's quiet strength.

Their union marked the continuation of the promise, the next chapter in the story of a people chosen to carry God's blessing.

### Abraham's Final Years

As Abraham aged, he reflected on the journey that had brought him to this point. From leaving his homeland to the test on Mount Moriah, his life had been a tapestry of faith, obedience, and trust in God's plan. He saw the beginnings of the fulfillment of the covenant: a son who carried the promise, a land purchased as a foothold in Canaan, and a family united by faith.

Abraham passed away at the age of 175, full of years and faith. Isaac and Ishmael came together to bury him in the cave of Machpelah, a moment of reconciliation and honor for the father they both loved.

### Isaac's Role as Patriarch

With Abraham's passing, Isaac assumed the role of patriarch. The covenant now rested fully on his shoulders, and he carried it with quiet resolve. Guided by the lessons of his father and his own experiences, Isaac began to lead the family, trusting in the God who had provided on Mount Moriah and beyond.

Isaac's leadership was marked by faith, patience, and a commitment to the promise that had shaped his family's history. He continued to build altars, offer prayers, and steward the land, always mindful of the covenant that bound him to the Creator.

**Closing the Chapter**

The continuation of the promise was a testament to Abraham's faith and God's unwavering faithfulness. Though Abraham's journey had come to an end, the covenant lived on through Isaac, ensuring that the legacy of trust, obedience, and divine provision would endure for generations.

# Chapter Six

## The Enduring Legacy

### A Covenant Across Generations

The story of Abraham and Isaac did not end with their lives—it became the foundation of a covenant that would ripple across generations. Through their obedience and faith, the promise given by God was not only fulfilled but also expanded, shaping the destiny of their descendants and the world.

Isaac, as the heir of the covenant, carried forward the lessons of faith he had learned from his father. His life, though quieter than Abraham's, was a continuation of the mission: to trust in God's promises, steward the land of Canaan, and prepare the way for the nations that would come from his lineage.

### Lessons from Abraham's Faith

Abraham's journey set a standard for what it meant to walk with God. His faith was not without struggles or questions, but it remained steadfast. He left his homeland without knowing where he was going, trusted in God's promise of a son despite his advanced age, and passed the ultimate test on Mount Moriah.

From Abraham, future generations learned:

- **Obedience**: Trusting God even when His commands seemed incomprehensible.
- **Patience**: Waiting for God's timing rather than forcing their own solutions.
- **Faith**: Believing in the unseen and trusting that God's promises would come to pass.

His life became a testimony to the power of faith, one that continues to inspire people across cultures and beliefs.

### Isaac's Quiet Strength

Isaac's role in the covenant was less dramatic but no less important. He embodied a quiet strength, trusting in God's provision and carrying forward the legacy of his father. Isaac's willingness to submit to God's will, even on Mount Moriah, demonstrated his faith and trust in both God and his father.

As a patriarch, Isaac continued to build altars, offer sacrifices, and teach his family about the covenant. His marriage to Rebekah brought new vitality to the promise, ensuring that the lineage of Abraham would endure. Isaac's steady leadership provided a bridge between Abraham's groundbreaking journey and the growing family that would eventually become a nation.

### The Role of Rebekah

Rebekah's entrance into the story brought a fresh dimension to the covenant. Her faith and willingness to leave her homeland mirrored Abraham's own journey, making her a fitting partner for Isaac. Together, they raised Jacob and Esau, two sons who would play pivotal roles in the unfolding of God's plan.

Rebekah's determination and wisdom shaped the next generation, ensuring that the promise would continue through Jacob, who would later be renamed Israel. Her story highlights the importance of trust, courage, and the role of women in God's divine narrative.

### The Promise Multiplies

The descendants of Abraham and Isaac multiplied, as God had promised. From Jacob came twelve sons, the patriarchs of the twelve tribes of Israel. Each tribe carried the legacy of the covenant, their lives shaped by the promise of land, blessing, and divine purpose.

Though their journey was not without challenges—famines, slavery in Egypt, and wanderings in the wilderness—the thread of God's promise remained unbroken. The God of Abraham, Isaac, and Jacob proved faithful through every trial, reminding them of the covenant sealed on Mount Moriah.

### The Universal Blessing

The covenant was never meant for Abraham's family alone. God's promise that **"through your offspring all nations on earth will be blessed"** pointed to a greater fulfillment.

The story of Abraham and Isaac foreshadowed the ultimate sacrifice: the offering of Jesus Christ, a descendant of Abraham, who gave His life to redeem humanity. In Him, the covenant found its universal expression, extending God's blessing to all people, regardless of nation or tongue.

### Lessons for Today

The story of Abraham and Isaac continues to resonate because its themes are timeless. From their journey, we learn about:

- **Trust**: Believing in God's promises, even when the path is unclear.
- **Sacrifice**: Surrendering what we hold most dear, trusting that God's plans are greater than our own.
- **Provision**: The assurance that God provides, often in unexpected ways.

Their story challenges us to reflect on our own faith journeys, inviting us to trust in the Creator's purpose and promises.

### The Towering Legacy

Abraham and Isaac's lives are more than a story—they are a legacy. Their faith shaped nations, inspired prophets, and pointed to the fulfillment of God's ultimate plan. From the altars they built to the covenant they carried, their lives are a reminder of what it means to walk with God.

The phrase **"The Lord Will Provide"** remains a cornerstone of faith, a testimony to the God who calls, tests, and provides in ways beyond our understanding.

### Closing the Chapter

The legacy of Abraham and Isaac continues to inspire, offering lessons of faith, obedience, and trust in God's provision. Their story is a bridge between the ancient and the eternal, a testament to the enduring power of God's promises.

www.ingramcontent.com/pod-product-compliance
Lightning Source LLC
Chambersburg PA
CBHW060047050426

42448CB00012B/3143